DOG TRAINING

10 IMPORTANT TRUTHS EVERY DOG OWNER MUST LEARN FOR DOG OBEDIENCE

TIM JACOBS

CONTENTS

Dog Training   v
Introduction   vii

1. Understanding a Dog's Behavior   1
2. Health and Behavior – How are they Connected?   12
3. Getting Your Dog Used to a New Environment   16
4. What do Dogs Feel When They Move?   17
5. Purchasing Supplies   20
6. House Training   25
7. Keeping your Dog Safe and Trouble-free   29
8. Fun and Games with the Dog   32

Afterword   35

DOG TRAINING

10 Important Truths Every Dog Owner Must Learn For Dog Obedience

Tim Jacobs

INTRODUCTION

This book contains proven steps and strategies on how to make your pet Fido behave, obedient, and happy at the same time. If your kids or even you have some trouble managing your pets, don't fret because this training manual will surely help you out.

Each chapter is filled with all the information that you need in dog care and training. Topics such as the various pet supplies you should give them, understanding their behaviors, training them to be accustomed to a new environment, and creating fun and exciting games for your dog and your family.

This training manual is very easy to understand. I made sure that the explanations here are simple but very useful so that you will have a better time reading it.

Although this reading material is designed for kids aged 8 to 12, there are some concepts they may not easily understand and several activities that require parental supervision. I sincerely wish that you guide your little ones across the various pages of this book so that they will learn from it and enjoy what they are reading.

Before you move to the first chapter, my first piece of advice is to be calm and patient when handling your dogs. Their actions can sometimes be very rash and annoying, but it takes a good owner to make them behave.

Thanks again for downloading this book, I hope you enjoy and learn something from it!

1
UNDERSTANDING A DOG'S BEHAVIOR

Reading a dog's attitude can be a very tricky business. Since they cannot speak, owners have to interpret what they are saying through their actions and their barking. If one is not observant, you might misinterpret their behavior and attempt to correct the behavior leaving the underlying cause that will render the correction ineffective and potentially confuse your dog. Always remember that there is a reason behind those actions that you deem annoying.

Often when a dog "misbehaves" it is because it either has not correctly been shown what is desired, or they are attempting to seek your attention. Both of these causes are easily remedied, more when they are younger than when they are adults, however, nothing is impossible and with patience even old dogs can learn new tricks.

Training a dog does not happen overnight, and if you go into a training session with a limited amount of time, often the dog will not reach the desired goal by the end of the time. Make sure to set a time aside for training where you will not have to rush, and you will be surprised at how this relaxed attitude will allow the dog to relax. Enjoy their session and often learn the required material significantly faster than you had anticipated.

Here are the explanations of the most common dog behaviors.

Aggression

Aggression in dogs is often misunderstood. It is uncommon for a dog to be naturally aggressive, and any aggressive behavior should be quickly remedied. It is important to determine what the cause of the aggressive behavior is, just as it is important to determine what kind of aggression is being displayed.

Fear

Often aggressive behavior is based on fear. Fear aggression is often made worse by a dog's owner even though they are unaware of this. Often if a dog reacts aggressively towards another dog or a stranger, their owner is more likely to tighten the leash and tense up when the dog is in the same situation in the future. Dogs can feel their owner getting nervous, so they think they are right to be nervous and to fear the situation and, for this reason, react again.

This behavior can be handled by remaining calm and showing the dog there is nothing to fear. By remaining calm and talking to the dog in a calming manner, your dog is less likely to get that boost of fear. By talking to the stranger and slowly introducing them, or the dog in question, you can clearly show the dog there is nothing to fear; for this reason eliminating the behavior. Often this will need to be regularly repeated until the behavior stops, and the longer this behavior has been permitted to continue, the longer it will be to fix.

Food

Often food aggression can stem from a dog's desire to protect what they think is theirs. Rescue dogs can be particularly protective of their food as they have gone without and have not yet realized that they are to be regularly fed. Often people will try to avoid facing this issue by feeding their dog in a different room and not allowing anyone near the dog.

This avoidance enforces the bad behavior and should not be permitted. If the dog is aggressive when someone is near their food, it is important to make the dog realize that no-one will take their food. It is also important that the dog is not permitted to be aggressive in regards to food or anything else.

Feeding each piece of food to the dog by hand until the dog realizes that you are not going to take their food is a good way to start. Once the dog consistently accepts this, placing a few kibbles at a time into a bowl and then holding the bowl while the dog eats is a good second step. Once they are comfortable with that, pet the dog and let them know they are a good dog as they eat. After the dog is comfortable with all this, allowing the dog to eat normally should be allowed as long as they do not take a step backward. If they do, go back a step and just remember that the behavior did not develop overnight and, therefore, will take time to remedy.

To prevent this behavior, training a puppy to allow you around their food dish while they eat is important and can be as easy as a scratch after they start eating.

. . .

Dominance

Occasionally aggression will be based on the dog's desire to dominate the person or another animal. This aggression is unacceptable behavior in any dog. Further information is found in the category Dominance.

Barking

This behavior is a dog's main form of communication. Often they do this to react to things that see or hear, like a person jogging in front of your lawn, for instance. They do this when they sense something that alarms them, or to indicate a new arrival in their territory. However, there are also times when it will bark if it needs help or attention. Excessive barking, for example, is its way of sending a distress signal and its needs are not being met.

Dogs bark for many reasons. Some of the most common are:

Loneliness

Often dogs will bark when they are left alone. This behavior is called "separation anxiety." Dogs are pack animals and, for this reason, do not do well when they are left alone for hours on end. If left, they will call for attention or start exhibiting negative behaviors to get attention as any attention, even bad, is better than no attention.

This attention-seeking activity can be solved by enrolling your dog in doggy daycare, providing plenty of toys at home for your dog or maybe even leaving a TV or radio on for your dog while you are away.

If your dog barks when they are left in a different room when you go to bed, it is important that they stay in whatever room you put them in. Letting them into your room, giving them a treat, or playing with them is enforcing bad behavior. Tell them to be quiet and be firm. Allowing them to have a blanket and a toy in their kennel will give them something else to focus on. Although the learning period can be difficult, remember, if you stick with it, your dog will calmly go to bed when told and remain quiet throughout the night.

Strangers

Dogs will naturally warn their family if there is someone coming to the door, whether a friend or someone they do not know. This behavior can be difficult to control as it is instinctual. Correcting your dog with your voice can help with this, and staying calm when people come to the door will all help in preventing this behavior.

Other Dogs

Dogs will often bark at other dogs. Short, high-pitched barks are often let off during play, and it is just your dog saying "Let's play! Come play with me!" Other barks, which are deeper, more chesty and are paired with a tense back and often hair around their neck standing on end are your dog's way of threatening another dog. This behavior is very rude and should not be permitted. This behavior should be treated as though your dog is swearing at the other dog in question and a firm "no" should be used to stop this behavior.

Bites

There are many reasons a dog could bite and none of them are acceptable. Most bites result from aggression stemming from multiple sources. Sometimes, however, dogs will bite themselves, and this is a sure sign that there is something not right, and they should be seeing a vet.

When a dog seriously bites a person, it is often a death sentence for the dog and, as a result, should be taken very seriously. Avoiding putting your dog in situations where a bite could occur is just as important as is the training to prevent a bite in the first place.

Aggression-Based Biting

Aggression-based biting should not be permitted regardless of the cause. In the aggression segment, there is more information although in severe cases it is prudent to hire a professional trainer to help overcome this potentially dangerous situation.

Medical

Often when a dog chews on itself it is because of a medical issue, either something is missing in their diet, pain or discomfort. This chewing is a sign for the dog to see the vet. Occasionally, dogs will continue biting themselves long after they have been cured. This continuation is because the biting and chewing has become a habit. Distracting your dog with toys is an excellent way to prevent the dog from doing potential damage to itself.

Biting the Leash

Biting the leash is often seen as something that is amusing. This leash pulling is a very disrespectful behavior, and it is the dog's way of saying that they do not respect you. Pulling on the leash or playing with them is not appropriate and telling the dog to release while removing the leash from the dog's mouth is the correct course of action.

Chasing Their Tail

While this behavior is amusing and at times confusing. While most people will see this behavior as a dog simply playing, and often it can be just that. However, this is not always the case.

Tail chasing can be caused by loneliness and is often seen in young dogs and other mammals who have been taken away from their littermates too early and left alone. It is often seen paired with pacing and self-mutilation in the form of chewing in dogs, cats, and caged animals.

If you are concerned with your dog's tail chasing and feel it is more than just the dog playing, spending more time with your dog may resolve the issue. Although this may not resolve the issue if it has been continuing for some time as it is habit-forming.

Chewing

While chewing your favorite pair of shoes, the couch or your son's favorite teddy may be frustrating, it is often the reasons behind the chewing that need closer examination.

Puppies

This behavior usually occurs during a dog's puppy stage because they tend to chew on toys and other objects to ease the pain of that occurs when their new set of teeth grows. Toys such as rope toys, Nylabones, and Kongs are all excellent ideas to distract and redirect this behavior to a more suitable subject than your new shoes.

Adults

Chewing as an adult is a natural occurrence. Dogs can not brush their teeth and, therefore, chew to keep their gums strong and their teeth clean. It helps them to remove any leftover food pieces from their teeth. Just as with puppies, this can be safely redirected to toys appropriate for their size and chewing strength. Rottweilers require a larger, more durable chew toy than a Bichon Frise would. A quick walk down the dog aisle in your local pet shop will offer many options to keep your dog happy and your furniture safe.

Inappropriate Behavior

Chewing can also occur when dogs are experiencing anxiety or boredom. This behavior can become an undesirable characteristic when they start chewing on furniture sets, shoes, or even your hands and feet.

Inappropriate chewing should be fixed while they are still young as it is easier at this point. The first thing that you need to do is to make sure your home is safe. Household cleaners and dangerous chemicals should be placed in high places where they are out of reach. Hide objects that may spark their curiosity like wires, cables, shoes, or kid's' toys. Dogs should also have appropriate playthings so they won't chew on household items.

If this does not correct the behavior, attention could be

the cause, and this can be dealt with symptomatically at first by crate training them. This should be done only while you are out and ensuring that when you are home that you spend time with them. Crates come in handy because they are like a den and calm the dog. The dog also can not destroy your house while they are safely contained. They should never be used as a punishment nor as a place to put your dog when you are at home.

Another option would be to enroll your dog in doggy daycare. These locations provide attention and socialization in a safe environment for your dog.

Digging

Digging is something a lot of dogs do for multiple reasons. Some dogs like digging to bury things in the dirt while others dig to uproot moles and other small animals from their tunnels under the surface. Regardless of why your dog likes to dig, often this behavior is frowned upon, particularly in the rose garden.

Teaching your dog that they are not allowed to dig in the garden can be accomplished multiple ways. The standard way is to tell them no and to remove them from the situation. Often dogs will learn quickly and leave the garden alone.

Another option is to create a sandbox or a small raised garden for your dog to dig in. Many compulsive diggers relish in this option and will spend hours digging in their area while leaving the roses intact.

Dominance

Dominance with people or other animals is often

frowned upon in family dogs. Certain breeds are more inclined to this than others. For instance, a German Shepherd is a naturally dominant dog who requires a firm yet gentle hand to train them. If there is no strong leadership role in the dog's life, they will often take that role upon themselves. This lack of leadership can create a string of issues and can lead to aggression.

Dominance in and of itself is not aggression. Dogs are pack animals and in a pack there is a leader and then a very particular pecking order. This order, in a family unit, should have the parents at the top, children in the middle and then the dog below them. It is never appropriate for a dog to challenge a child for dominance and should this happen; outside help may be required.

Eating Grass

Dogs all over the world eat grass, and there are many thoughts as to why this is.

Boredom

When dogs are bored, they eat. If they do not have food available, they will eat what is available and in the yard what is available is grass. This can be prevented with toys, exercise and time playing with your dog.

Lacking Diet

Occasionally dogs will eat grass when there is something missing from their diet. This is something to discuss with your veterinarian, and they may move Fido over to a high-fiber food to satiate their need.

Upset Stomach

Some veterinarians believe that dogs will eat grass to settle an upset stomach, much in the way you would take tums. If this is thought to be the case, it is important that your dog see a veterinarian to determine the cause.

2

HEALTH AND BEHAVIOR – HOW ARE THEY CONNECTED?

Similar to what happens to humans when they get sick, your furry pal's mood and behavior can also change based on their health. Parasites, diet program, and diseases are just some of the factors that can greatly affect their behavior. The pain and discomfort caused by ailments can result in a very negative attitude that is why owners need to take them to the vet regularly.

For example, if you notice that it is soiling and urinating numerous times in small quantities, your pet may have kidney problems or urinary tract infection. If this happens, you better take some samples of its urine or feces and send it your trusted vet immediately. The samples can provide a simple analysis of the situation. However, there are also instances when you have to take Fido to the hospital to get detailed information using X-rays and MRIs. When visiting the vet, you must tell every behavioral change that you noticed over the past few days so that it can assess the situation accurately.

Attitudes like fearfulness or aggression can trigger when a dog has hypothyroid disease. This is quite common in breeds like the Doberman Pinscher, Golden Retriever, Great Dane, Dachshund, and the Boxer. To keep their behavior in check, you can consult a pet nutritionist and ask for a diet that has a low dose of thyroid medication.

If your dog is always feeling irritated and has skin problems, it might be experiencing a tapeworm infestation. Checking their feces can easily identify this type of problem. If you see some moving white stuff that looks like rice grains in their droppings, those are tapeworms. Bring the samples to your vet and ask the right medication from them.

Hyperactive Behavior

Often hyperactive behavior is brought on by the lack of an appropriate outlet for their energy. Often these dogs require longer walks, more play time and often a job to do. This is particularly true of working dogs, both hunting, and herding. These dogs were bred for generations to be very active, be very intelligent and to work. Often the life of a pet is incredibly boring to these dogs and to prevent this from becoming undesirable behaviors activities such as agility, tracking, herding and other sports can be taken up. These will provide time for you to bond with your dog, for them to learn a new skill, and for both of you to become happier with their newfound outlet.

Jealousy

Jealousy can happen in dogs just as it can with children. With children, you often see this when a new baby is born. The child may revert to wanting to nurse, to wear diapers or they may become more whiny than usual. As with children, you need to understand that adding a new family member, be it human or animal, is a huge change for your dog. Making sure to set aside some time to allow alone time with the dog is one way to help this. Any aggressive behavior should be instantly dealt with and made very clear that such behavior will not be tolerated. This phase will pass and eventually the new member will be accepted into their family, and all will return to normal.

Panting

When a dog pants there are often multiple reasons. Often they can be linked to heat or stress.

Heat

Panting is a dog's main method of regulating their temperature. They only sweat through the pads on their feet, so a bulk of their body heat is expelled from their mouth through panting. This heat control is also accomplished through the hot moisture evaporating off of the tongue.

Stress

Panting is also a sign that the dog is stressed. This is often displayed in situations such as the vet's office, when meeting new people or possibly when they are being groomed. You will notice their body language will change, their ears and tails will be down, they will often lick their mouth frequently and may even shake. Stressed dogs are more likely to act out and to become aggressive in defense and for this reason caution should be taken to calm the dog without pushing them to avoid a potential bite.

To reduce stress in your dog's life you can:
Increase their exercise
Allow them toys to play with
Gently pet them in long, calming strokes
Redirect their attention
Develop a routine

3
GETTING YOUR DOG USED TO A NEW ENVIRONMENT

At some point in your life, you might need to relocate or move to another house. When owners move to a new home, they tend to bring their pets along to relieve stress. A key, to having a successful transition, is to keep your dogs in check while moving out.

While it is stressful for a dog to relocate, it is far less stressful for them to move, even internationally than it is to be rehomed. Rehoming your dog removes everything that is familiar to them and causes a large amount of stress, occasionally more than older dogs can handle.

4

WHAT DO DOGS FEEL WHEN THEY MOVE?

Your fluffy pals feel stressed when you transport them to another location. The unfamiliar territories that they see and the new neighbors that they'll meet can make them feel uneasy. This may lead to bad behaviors that were not present in them before.

Pets absorb their caregiver's emotions. If you feel anxious, they'll become jumpy and super sensitive to sudden bumps and squeaks around them. Displaying signs of being chaotic and scattered will make them feel insecure.

When moving, the owner must display a calm and assertive behavior so that your dog will be the same.

Stay Consistent

As much as possible, owners should keep most of their daily routine to keep the dogs acclimatized to your new place. Make sure to maintain the same schedule for feeding, walks, playtime and bedtime. If it is used to enter in a doggy door, provide one in your new place.

· · ·

KEEP his Favorite Items

Just because your apartment is new, it does not mean that you should also buy new toys for Fido. Dogs are sentimental to their belongings so make sure that you bring them along. Put the toys, bed, food and water trays in familiar spots so they will feel more in control and at home easily. Their diet should also be similar as to what they have before.

EXPLORE your New Environment Together

If you want your dog to learn to love the place, don't let it figure things out on its own. Instead, teach it the things yourself.

The first thing that you have to do is to take it for a brisk walk to introduce it to the neighborhood. Owners must be the one to lead the dog in walks and not the other way around. Walk your companion animal with a loose leash, and correct it if it starts to pull. Allow it to sniff in various places but make sure that you will be the one to decide where and when it will sniff. When going in and out of your place, be the first one to enter to show that you are the leader of the pack.

Being a competent and calm leader is vital in a human-animal relationship will help your dog make the right decisions. Be calm and patient so that your pet will be more willing to follow you.

TIPS ON ROAD Trips

Traveling with a furry companion can be fun and exciting if one is well-prepared for the journey.

The first thing to remember is to avoid risky driving. Pets

should stay at the back of the vehicle and away from the steering wheel. Don't give them any food or water while driving at the same time. In addition, dogs must be properly restrained using a harness attached to the seat belt or a crate to prevent them from distracting you while driving and also to protect everyone in an accident.

Don't forget to take your dogs on short breaks for potty breaks and a bit of exercise. Making them stretch their legs for a few minutes will make them tired, allowing them to relax more on the remainder of the journey.

If you need to sleep in a temporary room, find pet-friendly places where they can roam around and interact with other dogs. This will help exhaust their stored energy making them more relaxed at night.

When traveling on a plane, it is common practice to give the dog a tranquilizer either by injection or pill. Although it is effective to calm them down, some dogs don't react positively to this kind of treatment. They become more anxious because they lose control over their body. To find the best way to calm them down during long flights, consult your veterinarian first before you ride an airplane.

5

PURCHASING SUPPLIES

Aside from your love, time, and affection, pet dogs also need important material items to make them feel happy. Supplies such as medicine and proper dog food will help keep them in top shape. They also need toys to learn how to socialize with others. Below is a list of the most important supplies that you should purchase for your dogs.

Tagged Collar

No pet owner should ever let their dogs wander in the neighborhood without putting their collars at first. This tiny necklace will help strangers identify the dog's owner if ever it gets lost somewhere. These days, these items have become more useful thanks to technology. Some brands offer collars that have a tracking system. With just a few taps from your smartphone or tablet, you can pinpoint your pet's exact location or will notify you if Fido strays too far away.

When choosing a collar, be sure that it is not too tight. You have to change it once in a while as Fido grows up. To check if the dog's collar is too tight, your finger should easily slide between your dog's collar and its neck at all times.

Crate or Bed

Every dog must have his personal space at home in the form of a crate or bed. A well-crafted bed should provide adequate joint support for the pet. This is important because dogs tend to have joint problems when they grow old. It should be large enough for the animal to spread its legs and stretch out. The bed should also be cushioned evenly.

Nail Trimmers

Broken and split nails can be very painful for your pet that is why you need to trim its nails every four to six weeks. The most common, yet effective type of trimmer on the market is the one that looks like pliers. When you cut their nails, don't cut the quick. The quick is the portion of a dog's nail that is tender and soft. It is very painful to cut it out, and it might bleed, causing infections. To be safe, just cut 1/8 inch from the nail tips.

Grooming Brush

Breeds that have a long, thick coat, like Border Collies, Golden Retrievers, or Tibetan Mastiffs, are prone to getting their fur tangled. Brushing untangles their fur and keeps it clean from small and harmful debris.

The brushes required change depending on the breed you own. Long-haired breeds require a longer bristle and may require two or three different brushes. Short-haired breeds such as a Labrador Retriever would do well with a shedding blade as well as a finishing brush.

How the dog is brushed depends largely on their hair type, length, and cut. Researching the breed you own and speaking to their groomer will teach you how to groom your dog most effectively.

First Aid Kit

A first aid kit for your dog should contain the following main items:

- Information about pet first aid – This can be a book or any reading material that contains instructions on how to spot and identify symptoms and apply the proper first aid treatment.
- Contact information of people who can provide help – List the phone numbers of people you or anyone else left caring for your dog can call during emergencies. These people include your veterinarian, the emergency veterinary clinic, and the poison control center's hotline.
- Identification and health documents – Inside a waterproof bag, put important documents that contain your dog's health information. This includes your dog's vaccination records, a picture of your pet, and any other medical information about your pet.
- Nylon leash
- Bandages – The stretchable and self-clinging type is preferable it does not pull on your dog's fur. Different sizes and types are available at pet stores and is commonly referred to as "vet wrap."
- Muzzle – This is simply to keep them from hurting or biting others in case they get frenzied for some reason. It is not advisable to use this when your dog is having breathing problems, are choking, or is experiencing bouts of vomiting.
- Scarf - this is to cover the dog's eyes if they are panicking to help calm them.

Here is a checklist of other basic first-aid supplies:

- Gauze pads
- Adhesive tape
- Ice pack
- Hydrogen peroxide
- Rectal thermometer
- Petroleum jelly
- Antibiotic cream
- Witch hazel
- Penlight
- Glucose paste – good for diabetic dogs that have low blood sugar.

Toys

Toys are great objects to help Fido burn some energy. Playing keeps them fit and entertained leading to a positive attitude at home. It also strengthens their teeth and reduces dental deficiencies. Choose toys that are appropriate for their age and size. Avoid buying objects that have sharp edges or small parts to prevent them from harm. Giving them a multitude of objects may become too overwhelming for them so try to give your dog only a few toys at a time. They usually don't get bored with it for a long time, but if they do, replace it with another one.

Leash

If you are living in a state that has a leash law, then this is a necessity. A leash helps you keep them under control while walking in public areas. A 6-foot leash should be long enough for the animal to a couple of feet ahead of you without straining its neck.

Dog Food

Similar to humans, dogs are also omnivores, which

mean that they require meat and vegetables in their daily diet to meet their nutritional needs.

There are four main factors that determine the correct diet for Fido:

- Stage of life - puppy, adult, pregnant, nursing or senior.
- Level of Activity
- Health issues - both current and preventative such as obesity, diabetes, bladder stones and even eye or skin conditions.
- Breed size

A young Vizsla, for instance, requires a large breed dog food and a significant amount of it due to their energy levels. If you have a 9-year-old Chihuahua who spends most of its time sitting on your lap. Then it would only require a small amount of small breed food.

Packs of dog food labels usually have a guide regarding its suggested serving size, but it is only a general estimate. Only your veterinarian can give you suggestions that are appropriate for your dog and their individual needs.

6
HOUSE TRAINING

It takes more than just a stack of newspapers and doggy treats to keep them behaving inside your home. You need bucket loads of vigilance, commitment, patience, and most of all, consistency in order to house train your furry companions.

If you want to live a harmonious relationship with your pup, you have to accept the fact that they will have an accident in the house. Especially if they are puppies that are highly curious about their new environment and a small bladder. However, if you want to minimize these occurrences, consistent training from a very early age is necessary.

Below is a list of tips that you should follow to have a well-behaved puppy:

BUILD A ROUTINE.

Puppies work best when they are introduced to specific patterns on when it can eat, play or go to the potty.

Puppies should be taken out after every meal, after

waking up or after playing. These are times where your dog is likely to be in need of using a washroom and will often go within 30 minutes of these activities.

Take them for walks.

Since they are still little, these should be brief and frequent. Long walks, particularly with long-backed dogs, such as a Basset Hound, can injure their backs if they are taken for extensive walks too early. Walking provides activity and can strengthen its body and establish its bond with you at a very young age.

Find a bathroom spot outside.

This can be near trees or a patch of grass outside your house. When your puppy wants to go potty, take it there with its leash on its neck. So that it'll know what to do, you can utter a phrase like "go potty" before it eliminates its waste. When you do this outside your backyard, make sure that it doesn't go potty in front of your neighbor's lawn. Just find a nearby tree or empty patch of the lot where it can relieve itself. Afterward, pick it up and place it in a clean plastic bag.

Don't forget the rewards and prizes.

Whenever your pup manages to eliminate its waste on its designated spot outside, praise the dog or reward it with treats. It is important to reward them immediately, and treats should be given sparingly as it is important that your dog does not expect treats every time they are to go to the washroom. It is important to make sure that they are really done eliminating. They easily get distracted, and if you praise too soon, the puppy might not be able to finish what it is doing and may make a mess inside your house.

Be consistent with their feeding schedule

If your pet's feeding schedule is consistent, chances are it's potty business will also be the same. Puppies need to eat three or four times a day depending on their age, size, and genetic predispositions.

Put away your puppy's water dish before it sleeps

Do this two hours before its actual bedtime to reduce the risk of going to the potty during the night. Puppies can sleep for 7 hours without the need to eliminate once they reach the age of six to nine months. If your dog does wake you up in the middle of the night, just take it out to let it do its business. It is important not to play with your puppy because it could confuse them, and they may find it difficult to go back to sleep.

Confine your puppy in an enclosed space

Crate training should never be considered a punishment nor used in place of proper monitoring. Crates are an excellent way to provide your dog with the security and a place to call their own. Dogs will not soil nor wet the area where they sleep unless necessary and, as a result, will not make a mess in the crate. This should be large enough for the dog to stretch out and turn around in comfortably.

If your puppy has an accident in the crate, they will not

be particularly happy, yet your carpets will remain safe and clean.

An important fact that owners have to keep in mind is that most puppies are often older than six months before they are reliably house trained. Often they are consistent in the house within a couple months however accidents can happen. But with patience and consistency, they will learn quickly.

7

KEEPING YOUR DOG SAFE AND TROUBLE-FREE

Dogs become highly aggressive when they are being irritated by their surroundings. Most of the time, kids get hurt when interacting with their pets because they don't know how to respect its boundaries. If you want Fido to have a nice attitude when around people, you need to learn how to treat it with respect.

Below are some pieces of advice that you may want to share with your kids.

- Never touch their food – Although food aggression should not be tolerated, purposely irritating a dog by taking their food may upset your dog. This precaution is particularly true of young children as they are most likely to get bitten.
- Never steal their toys – Teaching children to respect a dog's toys is important. Just as the children would not want the dog taking their toys, they should learn that taking a dog's toys is unacceptable. Regardless, keeping an eye on

your dog is important in this situation to ensure the dog remains calm.
- Keep the kids away from the dog's sleeping area – Nobody wants to be disturbed when they sleep. Unlike humans, puppies don't have the option to lock their doors when children barge in their sleeping quarters uninvited. Put your pet's crate or bed in a silent location where it can sleep in peace yet accessible from the main living area so they know they can retreat there if they need to be alone.
- Avoid roughhousing – Children should not ride their pets no matter how big the animal is. In addition, they should not pull its tail or ears. They should also avoid screaming in front of their pets because it might react to the loud noise in a violent manner.

APPROPRIATE INTERACTION between Child and Dog

Once the young ones learn how to be polite and be more respectful to their furry friends, you can now teach them the proper ways to interact with them.

The first trick that you can teach them: fetch. It is a fun exercise that gives them the opportunity to share toys with the dog. If your pet is small, parents can give the leash to their kids and let them walk it for a couple of minutes. However, make sure that they only roam near the house, and you are with them to prevent any accidents.

Another way to build a strong kid and animal relationship is through responsibilities. If your child is old enough, assign them simple tasks like handing out the treats whenever Fido accomplishes something good. They can also assist in combing its hair or preparing its food. These activities will teach them how to groom properly and share their food with others.

Even at a very young age, toddlers can learn how to become great pack leaders. Together, you can practice giving commands like "Sit," "Stay," or "Off." These are simple yet very valuable methods that teach Fido to respect its young owner.

In addition, pets can also teach kids a few tricks. Enlist the help of your dog in encouraging young ones to learn about the parts of the body. Toddlers between the ages one and two can't speak yet, but they can be taught to identify where the eyes, nose, or ears are. Once they mastered a few parts by themselves, introduce them to new words such as fur, tail, or paws.

As an adult, it is your responsibility to ensure that your furry companions have a positive association with your kids and that everyone stays safe.

8

FUN AND GAMES WITH THE DOG

P laying and having fun is the ultimate way to remove your stress. The same can also be said with Fido. Doing some exciting activities with your pets can turn them into healthy and well-rounded animals that your family will surely love.

THE BENEFITS of Play

Here are the benefits, why extracurricular activities are good for both animal and owner:

- Keeps them in good physical condition – it helps keep your dog burn excess fat and makes the heart stronger. Moving around lubricates their joints and it also improves their sense of balance and coordination.
- Improves Mental Health – games that have rules will help exercise your pup's brain. These mental exercises will help them memorize commands

better and makes them more focused with the tasks they are doing.
- Makes them More Sociable – if they regularly play with other dogs or people, they will be able to improve their social skills. Dogs will learn how to behave properly, and the follow the rules.
- Bonding – Playing fetch for a few minutes every day improves an owner's and pet's bonding with each other.
- Relieve Stress - Even though you don't teach them how to be cute, dogs already have an innate knowledge of how to make their owners laugh. After a busy day of work, coming home with an eager pet will surely make you feel relaxed.

How to Play with Them

The most important thing, about playing with them, is that you are the boss who decides what game to play and set the rules. This control will help strengthen your image as the pack leader. You will also be the one to decide when to start and stop playing.

If you want to introduce a new game, make sure to start slowly until your pet understands the rules well. In addition, be sure that it fully grasps the game concepts before you move on the next one.

When your dogs become too excited or difficult to manage, take a break and wait for your pet to calm down.

For every achievement that they do, you should reward them with praises, hugs, and treats.

When kids are playing with Fido, teach them not to get too

physical. Avoid activities like tug-of-war or wrestling because it encourages biting and an aggressive attitude. Never use clothes as part of the activities so that they won't learn how to destroy it.

What's the Right Kind of Game?

Games that test their speed and agility are the best forms of strenuous activities for them because it exercises their limbs. An example of this one is retrieving exercises where you have to throw a ball or Frisbee, and they will attempt to catch it. An intense game of hide and seek will greatly stimulate Fido's brain. Or if you have the extra time, why not set up an obstacle course with your kids?

If you want to teach the toddlers how to give proper commands, a nice game of Statue will do the trick. Ask them to say "Go Wild" and see how their pet reacts. If the animal gets excited, teach them to say, "Freeze," then ask them to say "Sit." Hand out the reward if Fido manages to do this properly.

AFTERWORD

Thank you again for reading this book!

I hope this book was able to help you and your kid have a better relationship with Fido.

Having a dog can sometimes be a hard and daunting task. They can be messy, annoying, and will often chew your stuff at home. There are also moments in which you totally know what they think and then suddenly, they became unpredictable again!

However, having a furry pet also has its benefits. They are affectionate little creatures that know how to return the love that you give them. They are loyal guards who will protect your home and your kids. When you are sad and lonely, they know the tricks that can put a smile back on your face.

In handling Fido, the most important thing to remember is to be calm and patient. Learning their behaviors and finding the best way to communicate with them will greatly help you in making them behave.

Just like human beings, pet also needs a lot of care and attention. They should have adequate checkups and a balanced meal so that they will be healthy and happy. Playing and doing some exercise with them will help strengthen their body and will help channel their energies to a positive output. That way, they won't become too destructive.

Let your kids participate in the dog training so that they can form a strong bond with your furry pets at a very young age.

Thank you and have a great time with your pets!

www.ingramcontent.com/pod-product-compliance
Lightning Source LLC
Chambersburg PA
CBHW050336120526
44592CB00014B/2208